TaiLorMade Books Presents

Little Cupcake's First Day

By Nataisha T Hill

This book is dedicated to my wonderful girls. Mommy loves you and prays that all your hopes and dreams come true. Always believe in God, stay true to yourself, and never give up.

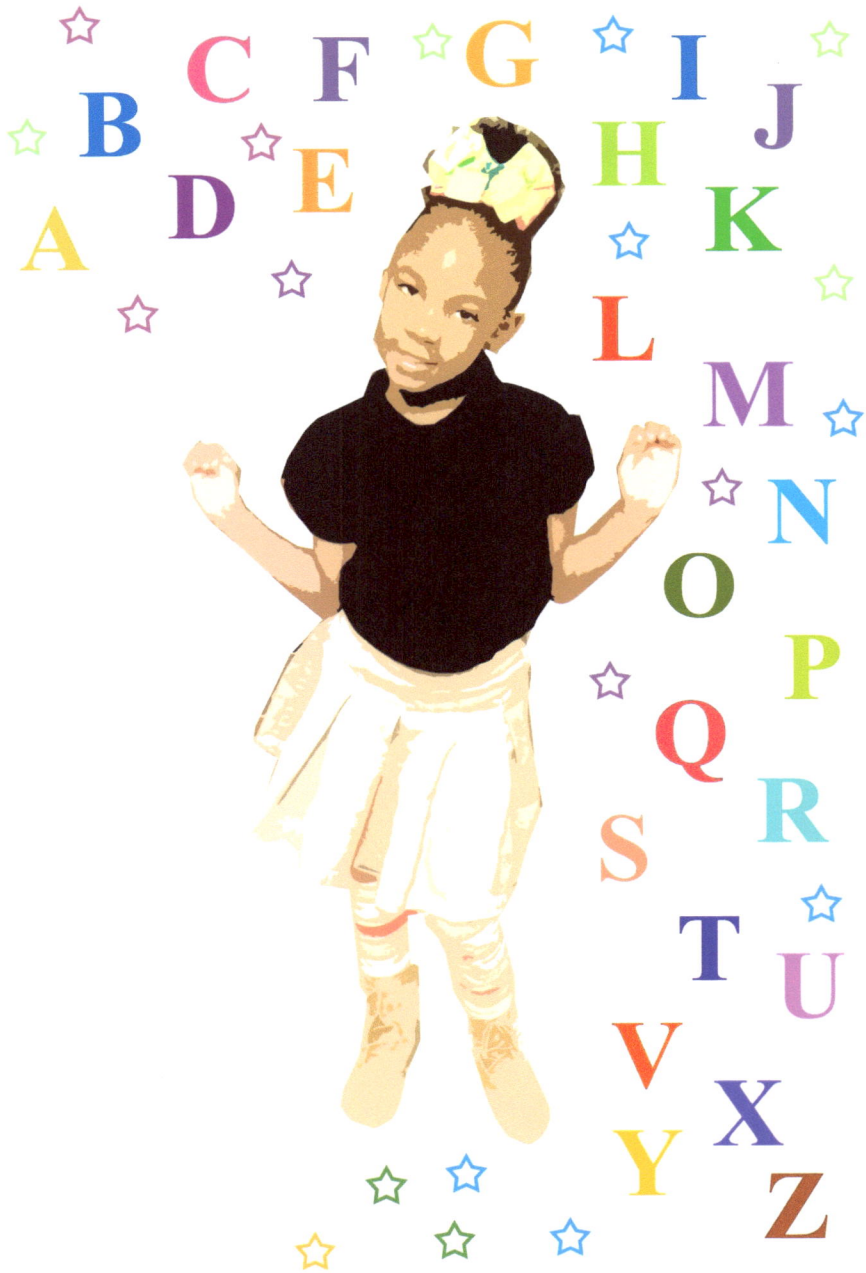

Wake up Little Cupcake!

It's time to go to school.

Where you'll learn you're A, B, C's,

And follow all the rules.

Sit down Little Cupcake!

Eat Breakfast before you play.

It will keep you feeling good,

And is the most important meal of

the day.

1 2 3 4 5 6 7 8 9 10

Purple White Gray

Pink Brown

Orange Black

RED SQUARE

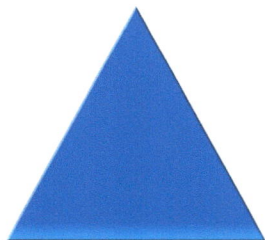

BLUE TRIANGLE

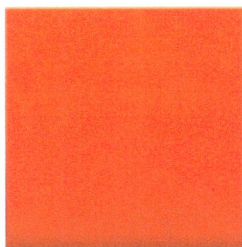

GREEN CIRCLE

YELLOW RECTANGLE

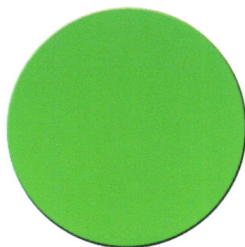

Listen Little Cupcake!

Pay attention to the teacher in class.

Practice your numbers, shapes, and

colors,

To make sure you do great and pass.

apple	banana	cherry(ies)	kiwi	peach(es)
pear	pineapple	lemon	watermelon	grapes
orange	melon	raspberries	plums	strawberry(ies)
tangerine	fig(s)	chestnut	mango	blackberries
red pepper	peas	broccoli	cabbage	lettuce
Potato(oes)	cucumber	garlic	cauliflower	carrot
tomato(oes)	leek	onion	mushrooms	pumpkin

Follow directions Little Cupcake!

Play well with others during recess.

Eat your vegetables and fruits at

lunch,

In order to stay alert and do your

best.

Welcome home Little Cupcake!

Do your homework right away.

Let Mommy help you go over it,

And then you can go and play.

Come in the house Little Cupcake! Let's practice saying ma'am and mister.

Then we can all get together and play with your little sister.

Time for dinner Little Cupcake!

We can't let it get too late.

You have to take your bath and put

on your pajamas,

After you get a happy plate.

Time for bed Little Cupcake!

Now let's bow our heads and pray.

Let's thank God for our family and

friends,

And that He blesses us with another

day!

Be Sure to Visit:

www.imadethebook.com

Thank You!

www.ingramcontent.com/pod-product-compliance
Lightning Source LLC
Chambersburg PA
CBHW041806040426
42448CB00001B/54